MW00773001

HeLPING OUT
and StayinG Safe

The Empowerment Assets

by Pamela Espeland and Elizabeth Verdick

free spirit
PUBLISHING®

Helping kids
help themselves™
since 1983

Library of Congress Cataloging-in-Publication Data
Espeland, Pamela
    Helping out and staying safe : the empowerment assets / by Pamela Espeland and Elizabeth Verdick.
        p. cm. — (The "Adding assets" series for kids ; bk. 2)
    Includes index.
    ISBN 1-57542-161-5
    1. Child development—Juvenile literature. 2. Social acceptance in children—Juvenile literature. 3. Self-esteem in children—Juvenile literature. 4. Helping behavior in children—Juvenile literature. 5. Safety education—Juvenile literature. I. Verdick, Elizabeth. II. Title.
    HQ767.9.E72 2004
    305.231—dc22   2004013171

At the time of this book's publication, all facts and figures cited are the most current available. All telephone numbers, addresses, and Web site URLs are accurate and active; all publications, organizations, Web sites, and other resources exist as described in this book; and all have been verified as of May 2006. The author and Free Spirit Publishing make no warranty or guarantee concerning the information and materials given out by organizations or content found at Web sites, and we are not responsible for any changes that occur after this book's publication. If you find an error or believe that a resource listed here is not as described, please contact Free Spirit Publishing. Parents, teachers, and other adults: We strongly urge you to monitor children's use of the Internet.

Search Institute® and Developmental Assets® are registered trademarks of Search Institute.

The original framework of 40 Developmental Assets (for adolescents) and the Developmental Assets for Middle Childhood were developed by Search Institute © 1997 and 2004, Minneapolis, MN 1-800-888-7828; www.search-institute.org. Used under license from Search Institute.

The FACTS! (pages 8, 21, 35, and 48) are from *Coming into Their Own: How Developmental Assets Promote Positive Growth in Middle Childhood* by Peter C. Scales, Arturo Sesma Jr., and Brent Bolstrom (Minneapolis: Search Institute, 2004).

Illustrated by Chris Sharp
Cover design by Marieka Heinlen
Interior design by Crysten Puszczykowski
Index by Ina Gravitz

10 9 8 7 6 5 4 3 2
Printed in the United States of America

Free Spirit Publishing Inc.
217 Fifth Avenue North, Suite 200
Minneapolis, MN 55401-1299
(612) 338-2068
help4kids@freespirit.com
www.freespirit.com

Free Spirit Publishing is a member of the Green Press Initiative, and we're committed to printing our books on recycled paper containing a minimum of 30% post-consumer waste (PCW). For every ton of books printed on 30% PCW recycled paper, we save 5.1 trees, 2,100 gallons of water, 114 gallons of oil, 18 pounds of air pollution, 1,230 kilowatt hours of energy, and .9 cubic yards of landfill space. At Free Spirit it's our goal to nurture not only young people, but nature too!

green press INITIATIVE

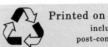

Printed on recycled paper
including 30%
post-consumer waste

Contents

Introduction

If you knew ways to make your life better, right now and for the future, would you try them?

We're guessing you would, and that's why we wrote this book. It's part of a series of eight books called the **Adding Assets Series for Kids.**

What Are Assets, Anyway?

When we use the word **assets**, we mean good things you need in your life and yourself.

We don't mean houses, cars, property, and jewelry— assets whose value is measured in money. We mean **Developmental Assets** that help you to be and become your best. Things like a close, loving family. A neighborhood where you feel safe. Adults you look up to and respect. And (sorry!) doing your homework.

There are 40 Developmental Assets in all. This book is about adding four of them to your life. They're called the **Empowerment Assets** because they're about feeling important and safe. When you have these assets, you know that you matter in the world. You're somebody, not a nobody. You help out and make a difference. You feel safe from harm instead of scared.

The Empowerment Assets

Asset Name	What It Means
Community Values Children	You feel that adults in your community value you and appreciate you.
Children as Resources	You are included in decisions at home and in your community.
Service to Others	You have chances to help others in your community.
Safety	You feel safe at home, at school, and in your neighborhood.

Other books in the series are about the other 36 assets.* That may seem like a lot, but don't worry. You don't have to add them all at once. You don't have to add them in any particular order. But the sooner you can add them to your life, the better.

Why You Need Assets

An organization called Search Institute surveyed hundreds of thousands of kids and teens across the United States. Their researchers found that some kids have a fairly easy time growing up, while others don't. Some kids get involved in harmful behaviors or dangerous activities, while others don't.

---

* If you're curious to know what the other assets are, you can read the whole list on pages 63–64.

What makes the difference? Developmental Assets! Kids who have them are more likely to do well. Kids who don't have them are less likely to do well.

Maybe you're thinking, "Why should I have to add my own assets? I'm just a kid!" Because kids have the power to make choices in their lives. You can choose to sit back and wait for other people to help you, or you can choose to help yourself. You can also work with other people who care about you and want to help.

Many of the ideas in this book involve working with other people—like your parents, grandparents, aunts, uncles, and other family grown-ups. And your teachers, neighbors, coaches, Scout leaders, and religious leaders. They can all help add assets for you and with you.

It's likely that many of the adults in your life are already helping. In fact, an adult probably gave you this book to read.

How to Use This Book

Start by choosing **one** asset to add. Read the stories at the beginning and end of that chapter. The stories are examples of the assets in everyday life. Then pick **one** idea and try it. See how it goes. After that, try another idea, or move on to another asset.

Don't worry about being perfect or getting it right. Know that by trying, you're doing something great for yourself.

The more assets you add, the better you'll feel about yourself and your future. Soon you won't be a kid anymore. You'll be a teenager. Because you have assets, you'll feel and be a lot more sure of yourself. You'll make better decisions. You'll have a head start on success.

We wish you the very best as you add assets to your life.

Pamela Espeland and Elizabeth Verdick
Minneapolis, MN

A Few Words About Families

Kids today live in many different kinds of families.

Maybe you live with one or both of your parents. Maybe you live with other adult relatives—aunts and uncles, grandparents, grown-up brothers or sisters or cousins.

Maybe you live with a stepparent, foster parent, or guardian. Maybe you live with one of your parents and his or her life partner.

In this series, we use the word **parents** to describe the adults who care for you in your home. We also use **family adults**, **family grown-ups**, and **adults at home.** When you see any of these words, think of your own family, whatever kind it is.

Community Values Children

What it means: You feel that adults in your community value you and appreciate you.

Jane loves to spend time at Uncle Joey and Aunt Rita's home. For one thing, they have a big, loud family and lots of pets. There's always something happening, and she's always welcome to join in. For another thing, there's Cousin Angelica—tall, beautiful, kind, and 18.

It's great to have an older cousin to do stuff with. Angelica has her driver's license and often invites Jane along for rides in the car.

There's only one problem, and his name is Curtis.

Curtis is Angelica's new but not-so-nice 21-year-old boyfriend. He calls Jane "The Pain" or "The Vain," depending on his mood. He's always saying things like, "Get lost, kid." Angelica usually responds with, "Curtis, behave." He may back off for a moment and say, "Just kidding," but he doesn't sound like he really means it.

Jane wants to say something to Angelica, but what? She doesn't want her cousin to think she's a baby or can't take a joke. "Maybe I shouldn't spend so much time at Uncle Joey and Aunt Rita's," she thinks. "Even though I'll miss them—and Angelica—a lot."

Over the next few weeks, Jane only goes over to her cousin's house a couple of times. When Angelica calls to ask, "Where've you been?" Jane says, "Oh, you know, busy with school and stuff." She hates lying this way, and she feels sad and empty inside.

Jane thought she had the *Community Values Children* asset, but now she's not so sure.

Think about your own life. Do you feel valued and appreciated by adults in your community?

If **YES,** keep reading to learn ways to make this asset even stronger.

If **NO,** keep reading to learn ways to add this asset to your life.

You can also use these ideas to help add this asset for other people—like your friends, family members, neighbors, and kids at school.

Facts!

Kids with the *Community Values Children* asset:

✓ know they are unique and special

✓ feel less lonely and more connected to the people around them

✓ have fewer behavior problems

ways to Add This Asset

 **AT HOME**

Make a List. Being valued means that people appreciate you, listen to you, and care about your thoughts and feelings. What adults outside your family do this for you? Think about your teachers, neighbors, and

coaches. Think about your friends' parents, your religious leaders, and youth group leaders. Who looks out for you? Who pays attention when you talk? Who treats you with respect? Who smiles when they see you? These are the people who value you. Write their names on a list. *Then . . .*

Reach Out. Plan to do *one* thing about every name on your list. Let each person know that he or she is important to you. *Examples:* Write a note, send an email, make a phone call, or pay a visit. (Get your parents' permission to visit, or bring them along. Call ahead to arrange a time.)

Ask Your Parents If You Can Get a Mentor. A mentor is a caring adult who's willing to guide you, advise you, and spend time with you. He or she serves as a role model and may become a trusted friend. Many communities and religious organizations have mentoring programs. So do several national organizations, like Big Brothers Big Sisters, Boys and Girls Clubs, the YMCA and YWCA, and Communities in Schools. To find out more, give them a call (check your local phone book) or visit their Web sites. To learn more about mentoring in general, visit the National Mentoring Partnership site. There's a whole section on how to find a mentor, and a page where you can search for a program in your area by entering your ZIP code.

Check Them Out Online

* Big Brothers Big Sisters of America: *www.bbbsa.org*
* Boys & Girls Clubs of America: *www.bgca.org*
* Communities in Schools: *www.cisnet.org*
* National Mentoring Partnership: *www.mentoring.org*
* YMCA: *www.ymca.net*
* YWCA: *www.ywca.org*

Don't Put Up with Put-Downs. Even though they should know better, some adults don't show kids enough respect. Certain adults may be rude to you, ignore your questions and feelings, or put you down in other ways. If you know any adults who act like this, what can you do? Start by talking to a parent or another adult you trust. Ask for help handling the situation.

Value Your Community. Maybe you don't live in the perfect neighborhood. Guess what? Perfect places don't exist! Besides, there may be plenty of great things about where you live. Think of the faces and places you'd miss if you moved away. Think of ways to help make your community stronger and brighter. Even picking up litter while you're on a walk or a bike ride can make a difference.

AT SCHOOL

★ Does your school have a mentorship program? If it does, sign up. Encourage your friends to sign up, too. If it doesn't, try asking your school to start a program. You and your friends could go to a meeting of the PTA (Parent-Teacher Association), PTO (Parent-Teacher Organization), or school board. Be ready to talk about why you want mentors. Often, when kids ask for something they really want or need, adults say yes!

★ Does your school honor kids who make a difference? Not just the best students or athletes, but other kids who make your school a better place to be? Maybe there's someone who's always willing to help out. Someone who makes new kids feel welcome. Or someone who has a great all-around attitude. These kids may not be the "stars," but your school wouldn't be the same without them. Ask a teacher or your principal about starting a Student Recognition Awards program for kids like these.

 **IN YOUR NEIGHBORHOOD**

★ Get involved in one or more positive programs for kids. Bring a friend or two.

5 Positive Programs for Kids

1. Camp Fire USA. Fun programs and services for boys and girls build caring, confident youth and future leaders. *www.campfire.org*

2. Boy Scouts of America. Character development and leadership training for boys and young men. *www.scouting.org*

3. Girls Incorporated. Programs that inspire all girls to be strong, smart, and bold. *www.girlsinc.org*

4. Girl Scouts of the USA. Builds character and skills for success in girls and young women. *www.girlscouts.org*

5. Police Athletic Leagues (PAL). Athletic, recreational, and educational activities for kids. *www.nationalpal.org*

★ Read your community's daily newspaper for several days or a week. If you don't get it at your house, read it online at your school or local library. Look for articles written about

> **TIP:** Help out by sharing a positive story about someone you know.

kids. Are the articles mostly positive—or mostly negative? Do the kids seem mostly good—or mostly bad? Write a letter to the editor and describe what you found. If the articles are mostly negative, ask the newspaper to publish more positive stories about kids.

★ Be nice to the younger children you know. Smile and say hi when you see them. Take a few minutes to talk with them. Remember that little kids look up to older kids like you.

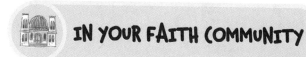

IN YOUR FAITH COMMUNITY

★ Notice the people in your faith community who work with kids. Treat them with respect. You might send a thank-you note or make a thank-you card for your religious school leader, your youth leader—who else? Showing your appreciation could really make that person's day.

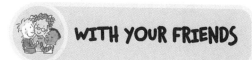

WITH YOUR FRIENDS

★ Think about how you act when you're out in public together—at the mall, at the park, or just walking down the street. Is your behavior something to be proud of? Does it show you and other kids your age in a positive way? Right or wrong, many adults will look at you and your friends and judge *all* kids by the way you act. Try to set a good example by not littering or using bad language. If you're walking in a group, make way for other people. Smile and say hi to the adults you meet.

Start Adding!

Pick at least ONE idea you've read here and give it a try. Then think about or write about what happened. Will you try another way to help adults in your community value and appreciate kids—including you?

Back to
Jane's
Story
Jane decides that it's time for her to speak up. One night, she invites Angelica over so they can listen to a new CD and hang out.

After a while, Angelica starts talking about Curtis—how cute he is, how great he is to her, the fun they have together. Jane listens to her cousin, then says, "I'm glad you like Curtis and he likes you. But I don't think he likes me very much. I think he kind of hates me."

Angelica looks at her in surprise. "Of course he doesn't hate you! He might say dumb stuff sometimes, but he's just being a guy, you know?"

"Actually, I *don't* know," Jane says. "Other guys don't act like that. I mean, Uncle Joey would never say those things, and neither would your brothers. I guess I'm saying that Curtis has a way of hurting my feelings."

"Wow," Angelica replies. "I never thought about it that way. I'm sorry, Jane. Is that why you haven't been coming around as much lately?"

When Jane admits that she's been avoiding Curtis, Angelica says, "I'm going to talk to him about this later tonight. If he can't be cool around you, he's not welcome when you're at my house—okay? And besides, my parents and brothers all really miss you."

Jane smiles and says, "Thanks. I miss them all, too." Then, in a joking way, she adds, "How could they *not* miss Jane the Vain?"

Children as Resources

What it means: You are included in decisions at home and in your community.

Kevin's Story

Kevin got his own library card way back on his fourth birthday. Ever since, he has loved going to the library. His foster dad usually brought him there at least once a week—until last week. That's when the public library closed for renovation.

19

Big changes will be made in the next several months. There are plans for more space and more books, a bigger reading room, and two new meeting rooms for grown-ups. Parents and teens will have a coffee shop they can go to. The little kids will get beanbag chairs and quiet toys in the new tots' section.

It's all good—except for one thing. Nobody seems to have thought about the in-between kids like Kevin, who are too young for the coffee shop but too old for the area meant for little kids.

"Hey!" Kevin thinks. "What about me and my friends? What new things will the library have for us?"

Kevin wonders why no one thought of asking him or his friends for ideas.

Kevin would like to have more of the *Children as Resources* asset.

Facts!

Kids with the *Children as Resources* asset:

✓ have higher self-esteem

✓ are more responsible

✓ feel more *competent* (able to do things well)

Think about your own life. Do you feel included in decisions at home and in the community? Do adults ask you what you think, want, and need?

If **YES,** keep reading to learn ways to make this asset even stronger.

If **NO,** keep reading to learn ways to add this asset to your life.

You can also use these ideas to help add this asset for other people—like your friends, family members, neighbors, and kids at school.

ways to Add This Asset

 **AT HOME**

Pitch in More. How helpful are you at home? (Be honest.) Running a home is a big job, and your dad or mom could probably use all the help they can get. *Examples:* Do your chores without being asked. Pack your own lunch in the morning, or set the table for dinner. Offer to baby-sit younger siblings or keep them busy when your parents are busy themselves.

Call a Meeting. Family meetings are a great way to get everyone involved in family decisions—kids included. If your family doesn't have regular family meetings, ask your parents if they're willing to give it a try.

6 Tips for Terrific Family Meetings

1. Set a starting time, ending time, and place for your meeting. *Example:* Every Thursday after dinner, from 7:00–7:30, at the kitchen table.

2. A few days before the meeting, put a piece of paper on the kitchen counter. Have family members write down things they want to talk about during the meeting. Bring the paper to the meeting. Use it as your *agenda*—your list of things to talk about and do.

3. Agree on a few simple ground rules in advance. *Examples:* Everyone gets a chance to talk. Everyone listens respectfully when someone else is talking. No whining or raised voices.

continued

4. Decide on a leader for each meeting. Everyone should get a chance to lead—not just the grown-ups.

5. Take turns talking. You might pass around a "talking stick." The person holding the stick gets to talk without being interrupted. A talking stick can be almost anything—a chopstick, a ruler, a wooden spoon. Or your family might want to make a fancy decorated talking stick.

6. Try to end the meeting on time so it doesn't drag on and on.

Get Creative. Instead of buying gifts for birthdays and holidays, why not make some? If you can't think of anything to make, come up with one-of-a-kind gift certificates. Write them by hand or print them out on a computer. *Examples:* A certificate good for ten hugs, or five times of cleaning the cat's litter box, or one breakfast in bed, or two hours of baby-sitting your little sister, or four times of taking the trash out, or a whole week of keeping your room neat without being asked or told.

Be a Planner. Ask if you can help plan the next big family event. Maybe it's your annual Fourth of July picnic. Or your winter break vacation. Or the family reunion that happens on Memorial Day weekend every five years (and you didn't know you had so many cousins!). Tell your parents that you want a useful job to do. *Examples:* For a picnic, maybe you could help plan the menu and do some of the cooking. For a vacation, maybe you could go to the library, look at some guidebooks, and make a list of fun places to visit and things to do. Be sure to write down the addresses, phone numbers, and days and hours when places are open. For a reunion, maybe you could help plan games and activities for younger kids.

Be a Teacher. Offer to teach your parents something they don't know. Maybe it's how to play a game you enjoy. Or something new you learned in school. Or a cool dance step. Or you could bring them up-to-date on the latest music.

AT SCHOOL

★ Find ways to be a decision-maker at your school. Run for office in your classroom, homeroom, or school. Volunteer to serve on the planning committee for Parents' Night or your school fair. Find out if kids are allowed to go to meetings of the PTA (Parent-Teacher Association) or PTO (Parent-Teacher Organization).

> **TiP:** Some schools have PTSAs (Parent-Teacher-STUDENT Associations) so kids can be more involved.

IN YOUR NEIGHBORHOOD

Share Your Skills. You're good at something—maybe many things. Find ways to share your talents and abilities with others. *Examples:* If you're a good reader, you could offer to read to younger kids at your school. Or volunteer to lead a read-aloud story hour at the library. If you're a computer wiz, go with a family grown-up to a senior citizens' home or center. Teach seniors there how to surf the Web. Or you might create a Web page for the home or center.

Think Big. Does your community allow kids to serve on important committees? Like the park board? The school board? Maybe even the town council? Some communities do. Ask your parents and teachers to help you find out. If kids are welcome, learn how you can get involved.

Help Plan a Block or Building Party. If your block or building has annual get-togethers for neighbors, find a way to help. *Examples:* Come up with games for younger kids to play. Offer to help with set-up or clean-up. Organize your friends into a set-up or clean-up team.

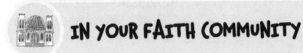

IN YOUR FAITH COMMUNITY

★ Find ways to lead and serve in your faith community. *Examples:* Is there a council or committee you can join? Can you help teach and care for younger children? Can you do a reading for a worship service?

A message for you

Just because you're young doesn't mean you have to sit quietly by while adults make all the decisions. Believe in **kid power!** It's YOUR home, YOUR school, YOUR neighborhood, and YOUR faith community, too. You have the right to be seen *and* heard.

WITH YOUR FRIENDS

★ If you and your friends go to the same school, talk about the problems you see there. Try to agree (or take a vote) on the one you think is the most serious. Then brainstorm some ideas for solving the problem. Share your ideas with your teachers or the school principal. If you and your friends don't go to the same school, identify a problem in your community. Find an adult who believes in your cause—a parent, youth group leader, or community leader—and ask that person to be a mentor to you and your friends. (For more about mentors, see page 10.)

Start Adding!

Pick at least ONE idea you've read here and give it a try. Then think about or write about what happened. Will you try another way to make sure you're included in decisions at home and in your community?

Back to
Kevin's
Story
Kevin talks with his foster dad about the library. "There's new stuff for teenagers and little kids, but nothing special for kids my age," he explains.

"You've got a really good point," says his dad. "And I think other people should hear it, too. There's a community meeting next Tuesday at seven o'clock. I'm planning to go. Why don't you come with me? Toward the end of the meeting, people will have a chance to comment. Can you write down some ideas between now and then?"

"Sure," Kevin says. "I'll get my class at school involved, too."

Over the next few days, Kevin thinks about ways to make the library better for in-between kids. He works with his class to make a wish list for the library, including everything from more new CDs to more books about skateboarding and horses.

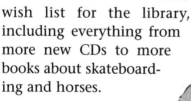

During the comments part of the community meeting, Kevin raises his hand. He waits to be called on, then reads the wish list. He explains that these aren't just his ideas, but also ideas from other kids in his class at school.

When he sees people nodding their heads, Kevin feels encouraged. He follows up by writing a letter to the editor of the community newspaper. His letter gets published in the paper! A few days later, the phone rings at Kevin's home. It's the head of the library board, and she wants to talk with Kevin.

"We like your ideas very much," she says. "Could you come to our next meeting and tell us more about them? Also, we're thinking about starting a first-ever kids' committee for the library. Would you want to be part of it?"

"I want to do both," Kevin says, "but I have to ask my dad if it's okay first." Kevin is pretty sure he already knows what his dad will say—yes, and double yes!

Service to Others

What it means: You have chances to help others in your community.

Kyoka's Story

Each year, Kyoka's school hosts an Amity Scholar. An Amity Scholar is a student who joins the school from another country and lives with a volunteer host family. Kyoka's family is having a special meeting to talk about maybe hosting this year's new student, a boy from Spain.

"It might be hard having a stranger live in our home," Kyoka says. "It will be like having company all day every day—and all night, too."

"The new student won't be a stranger for long," Kyoka's stepmom says. "I've heard that Amity Scholars often become family members. For you, Kyoka, it might be like getting a new brother—one close to your age."

"Will I have to share my toys?" Kyoka's little sister Mika wants to know.

"Not unless you want to," their dad says, smiling.

"When I was in high school," their stepmom says, "my best friend's family had a student from Austria live with them for a year. Sandy and Elsa are still close. They even visit each other with their husbands and children."

"Being a host family won't always be easy," their dad says. "But I think it will be a good thing to do. It's a way for us to reach out and help someone else."

"My teacher, Mr. Barnes, is always telling us a quote by Muhammad Ali, the famous boxer," Kyoka says. "It goes like this: 'Service to others is the rent you pay for your room here on earth.' Hosting an Amity Scholar is a service, isn't it?"

"It sure is," her stepmom replies.

Kyoka feels ready to try the *Service to Others* asset.

Think about your own life. Do you have chances to help others in your community? When you have those chances, do you act on them?

If **YES,** keep reading to learn ways to make this asset even stronger.

If **NO,** keep reading to learn ways to add this asset to your life.

You can also use these ideas to help add this asset for other people—like your friends, family members, neighbors, and kids at school.

ways to Add This Asset

 **AT HOME**

List What You Do. Sit down as a family and talk about how you're serving your community. Maybe your stepdad coaches the youth basketball team at the YMCA. Maybe your grandma delivers homemade meals to community members who can't cook for themselves. Maybe your family has a foster child. What else? Make a list of everything you do to help others. Hang it on your refrigerator or family bulletin board. Be proud of the ways your family serves.

Or . . .

Start Somewhere. If your family isn't serving yet, maybe *you* can be the one who inspires them to get started. Say that you want to help others in your community, and you'd love to do it as a family. This doesn't have to mean a huge commitment. Even one hour a week can make a big difference. Need some ideas? Go with a family grown-up to one or more of these places and ask what kind of help they need: (1) your local community or recreation center, (2) a nursing home or retirement center, (3) an animal shelter, (4) an educational program for young children, such as Head Start, (5) your place of worship.

Connect and Serve

With your family:

★ Check out a Volunteer Center. Volunteer Centers bring people and community needs together. There are centers in cities and towns across the United States. To find one near you, call 1-800-VOLUNTEER (1-800-865-8683). Or visit this Web site: *1-800-VOLUNTEER.org.*

★ Take part in National Family Volunteer Day. It's held each year on the Saturday before Thanksgiving. To learn more, contact your local Volunteer Center or visit this Web site: *www.pointsoflight.org.*

★ Visit Volunteer Match on the Web: *www.volunteermatch.org.* Enter your ZIP code and press "Search" to get a list of volunteer opportunities in your area. The ones that are best for families or groups are marked with a little brown "G" in your search results. Also look for ones marked "K" (for Kids).

Give a Little, Get a Lot. If your family isn't ready to volunteer time, you can serve in other ways. *Example:* Many grocery stores have a bin next to the exit so families may donate canned goods or packaged items to a local food shelf. This makes it simple to be of service each time you shop. *Another example:* Find an organization that collects used clothing, furniture, household items, and toys in good condition for families in need. Every month or two, look around your home for things to donate, then schedule a pickup. Or ask a parent to help you find the nearest drop-off center.

Share the Wealth. Maybe you have an allowance, or you earn money by doing odd jobs. Do you donate any of your money to causes you believe in? Give what you can—it doesn't have to be a lot.

TIP: Ask a family adult to help you find a cause (or causes) and make sure that your money will be put to good use.

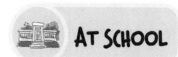

AT SCHOOL

⭐ Join the service club at your school. If your school doesn't have a service club, think about starting one. Call or visit other schools in your community to learn what kids there are doing. Or ask your friends, if they go to different schools.

5 Ideas for School Service Club Activities

1. Adopt-a-Hallway and pick up trash.
2. Help out in the school library or media center.
3. Help teachers in the classrooms.
4. Tutor other kids.
5. Raise money or collect donations (clothes, toys, books) for a local homeless shelter.

IN YOUR NEIGHBORHOOD

★ Think about the people you know in your neighborhood—on your block, in your apartment building, down the road, or across the street. Is there someone who could use your help? Maybe you could pull weeds in a neighbor's lawn. Or walk a neighbor's dog when you get home from school. Or help shovel snow in the winter. Talk with your parents about who you might help and what you might do.

★ Take part in a National Day of Service. This is a day when millions of people across the country—kids, teens, and grown-ups—take time to help others. It's fun and exciting to get involved.

5 National Days of Service

1. Martin Luther King Jr. Day. The third Monday in January. *www.mlkday.org*

2. National and Global Youth Service Day. The third weekend in April. *www.ysa.org/nysd*

3. Earth Day. Every year on April 22. *www.earthday.net*

4. Join Hands Day. The first Saturday of May. *www.joinhandsday.org*

5. Make a Difference Day. The fourth Saturday in October. "The national day of doing good." *www.usaweekend.com/diffday*

IN YOUR FAITH COMMUNITY

★ Almost all faith communities serve others. Find out what yours does and how you can get involved. If your faith community doesn't already have ways for kids to serve, talk with your youth leader, religion class teacher, or religious leader. You might suggest starting a Kids Care Club™. Clubs must be sponsored by a school, church, synagogue, community center, or other youth organization. To learn more, visit this Web site: *www.kidscare.org.*

 ## WITH YOUR FRIENDS

★ Service is more fun when you do it with a friend—or a whole group of friends. You might get together with your families and take part in a National Day of Service. You might join a service club that sounds cool to you. Or you might start your own service organization.

A message for you

Do you think you're too young to start a service organization? You're not! Lots of kids have started and run organizations that help people, the environment, animals, and more. You can read about some of them at *www.idealist.org/kt*. If they can do it, you can, too!

Start Adding!

Pick at least ONE idea you've read here and give it a try. Then think about or write about what happened. Will you try another way to reach out and help others?

Back to
Kyoka's
Story
"I'm kind of excited to help the Amity Scholar," Kyoka says. "I remember what it was like for me when I was the new kid at school. I felt lonely, but then when people tried to be my friend, I was happy. The new student will be far from home, and that will be really hard. We can help him feel welcome."

Mika adds, "I want to learn Spanish from him. It will be fun to have a pretend big brother!"

Both girls wait to hear what their parents will say next.

"Well," their stepmom says, "your dad and I have been wanting to do something to help your school. This is a really special way to do it."

"Yes," their dad says, "and we've got room. All kinds of room, in fact."

"What do you mean?" Kyoka wants to know.

"A spare room for the Amity Scholar to live in," he says, "*and* room in our hearts to make him feel at home."

"That's really corny, Dad," says Kyoka, rolling her eyes. But she's smiling, and everyone else laughs.

Tomorrow, Kyoka and her family will go to the school principal to tell her the good news.

Safety

What it means: You feel safe at home, at school, and in your neighborhood.

Reggie's Story

Reggie knows there are some unsafe areas in his neighborhood. For a while now, he's been picked on by older boys while walking home from school. At a house down the block, someone was arrested for dealing drugs. Sometimes, kids steal bikes or paint graffiti on the street signs and other places.

A few weeks ago, a neighbor's car alarm went off in the middle of the night. When she went out to turn it off, she saw that someone had broken into her car.

Even though this stuff goes on, Reggie doesn't want to stay indoors, hiding out. But the older he gets, the more his mom worries about letting him leave the house.

He thinks, "Why should I be the one stuck inside, when I'm following the rules and not doing any harm?"

Reggie believes he deserves to have the *Safety* asset.

Think about your own life. Do you feel safe at home, at school, and in your neighborhood?

If **YES**, keep reading to learn ways to make this asset even stronger.

If **NO**, keep reading to learn ways to add this asset to your life.

You can also use these ideas to help add this asset for other people—like your friends, family members, neighbors, and kids at school.

Facts!

Kids with the *Safety* asset:

✔ feel less worried and more safe

✔ are less *aggressive* (pushy and violent)

✔ get along better with others

ways to Add This Asset

 **AT HOME**

Know What You Would Do If . . . What would you do if a stranger called on the phone? Knocked on the door? Came up to you on the street? What would you do if your ride was late picking you up from a game?

If you got lost in the mall? If you smelled smoke in your apartment building? If a friend tried to get you to do something wrong? If someone you met on the Internet asked to meet you in person? Try to come up with as many "What would you do if . . . ?" questions as you can. Have family meetings to talk about them and decide what you would do.

Make Safety Plans. What would your family do in a fire? In another kind of emergency, like an accident, sudden illness, or poisoning? In a disaster (a flood, tornado, hurricane, or earthquake)? Have family meetings to talk about and make safety plans.

Be a SAFE KID. With your parents or another family adult, visit the National SAFE KIDS Campaign Web site: *www.safekids.org.* Download and print out their checklists on Fire Safety, Home Safety, Poison Safety, Water Safety, Halloween Safety, and more. Go over each checklist together to see how safe your home is. What can you do to make it safer?

Know "Stop, Drop, and Roll"

Most clothing is *flammable*—meaning it can catch on fire and burn. This can happen in a second if you get too close to a hot stove, a campfire, a lit match, or a barbecue grill. Memorize "Stop, Drop, and Roll" in case this ever happens to you.

★ *STOP* immediately. Don't panic or run.

★ *DROP* to the ground. Cover your face and mouth with your hands.

★ *ROLL* over and over to put out the flames.

If you do get burned, cool your skin with water. Then find a grown-up or call 911.

Know Gun Safety. If you see a gun in your home, a friend's home, or anywhere, do this: STOP. DON'T TOUCH. GET AWAY. TELL AN ADULT. Guns are the second leading cause of death for young people ages 19 and under in the United States. (Motor vehicle accidents are the first.) If your family has guns in the home, they should be stored safely—unloaded and locked up.

Have a Safe Place to Go. Everyone needs a safe place to go when they're upset, worried, or afraid. Find a place at home that works for you. This might be your bed, a closet, a tree house, a homemade fort, or a quiet corner any-where. Use the time alone to write in your journal or lis-ten to soft music. Think you're too old for a teddy bear or blanky? Lots of kids hold on to these security items well into their teens (or adult years)—and there's nothing wrong with that!

Talk About Your Fears. How often do you feel afraid? Hardly ever, sometimes, a lot of the time, or all of the time? What are you afraid of? Talk about your fears with your dad, your mom, or another adult you trust. Ask for their advice on ways to feel less scared and more safe.

A message for you

If you feel afraid a lot of the time or all of the time, your fears may be out of control. They may be keeping you from doing things you want or need to do—like meeting new people, going new places, or playing with your friends. Does it seem like fear is in charge of your life? Talk with an adult as soon as you can.

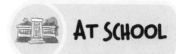 **AT SCHOOL**

★ Bullies are a big problem in many schools today. Lots of kids are afraid to go to school because of bullies. If you're bullied, or you see someone else being bullied, tell a teacher or your principal.

★ If school feels unsafe to you, tell your parents. Ask them to volunteer at your school so they can see for themselves what it's like.

★ Take a safety walk around your school with your class or club. Notice places or things that seem unsafe. Make a list and give it to your principal.

IN YOUR NEIGHBORHOOD

Make Your Home a McGruff House. A McGruff House is a temporary safe place for kids who are lost, hurt, threatened, or scared. Ask your parents if your home can be a McGruff House. They can learn more about what this means by contacting the National Crime Prevention Council. They can call 1-877-367-6646 (toll-free) or visit the Web site: *www.ncpc.org*.

> **TIP:** Being a McGruff House works best in a home where an adult is present most of the time. If both of your parents work full-time, this may not be right for your family.

Stay Away from Unsafe Places. If it feels funny or strange to you, don't go there. Take the long way around or take another route. Avoid places where there's no adult supervision. You're not being a scaredy-cat. You're being smart.

Report Problems You See and Hear About. For example, don't just ignore graffiti. Tell your parents or another adult so they can report it. Have you noticed a vacant lot full of trash? Is there another place in your neighborhood that seems scary or dangerous to you? Is there an animal you think is being abused? A kid who gets yelled at a lot? This isn't tattling or spreading gossip. It's helping to make your neighborhood safer.

IN YOUR FAITH COMMUNITY

★ How safe is your place of worship? For example, would everyone know what to do in case of a fire? Are all of the exits clearly marked? What if a tornado is heading your way? Is there a place where members can gather? Ask your religion class leader or youth leader if your congregation has safety plans in place. Your class could help out by taking a safety walk through the building and grounds. Write down anything that seems unsafe or in need of repair.

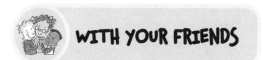

WITH YOUR FRIENDS

★ Watch out for each other. Don't tease each other to take dumb risks or do crazy things. Agree to stay safe together and help each other stay out of danger.

★ Listen to each other. If a friend talks about feeling unsafe, encourage him or her to tell a trusted adult. Don't promise to keep secrets when it comes to safety. Tell your parents what your friend told you.

Start Adding!

Pick at least ONE idea you've read here and give it a try. Then think about or write about what happened. Will you try another way to feel safer at home, at school, and in your neighborhood?

Back to Reggie's Story Reggie talks to his mom about how he's scared to walk home when he gets off the school bus. He's tried avoiding areas where the older boys hang out, but they always seem to find him anyway. They call him names like "crybaby," "wimp," and worse. He's asked them to stop calling him names, but that hasn't helped, either.

"Okay," his mom says. "It's time to get serious about this problem. Those boys are trouble."

Reggie's mom calls the school principal. Together, they come up with the idea of pairing Reggie with an older student who lives nearby. The student agrees to help look out for Reggie on the way home from school each day.

Reggie's mom has more ideas, though. At the next neighborhood meeting, she talks about two ways to make their neighborhood safer for everyone. Reggie comes along to hear what she has to say.

"First," she tells the group, "we should start a Neighborhood Watch Group. We'll need to contact the police department—they can help us set it up. Second, we should think about having at least one McGruff House in our neighborhood. A McGruff House is a safe place for kids who need help. Once we have a Neighborhood Watch Group, we can get this going, too."

After the meeting, as people are getting ready to leave, Reggie gives his mom a hug. "Way to go!" he says. "I'm proud of you."

"I'm not through yet," she says. "Next, we're going to find a way to clean up that graffiti."

A NOTE TO GROWN-UPS

Ongoing research by Search Institute, a nonprofit organization based in Minneapolis, Minnesota, shows that young people who succeed have specific assets in their lives—**Developmental Assets** including family support, a caring neighborhood, integrity, resistance skills, self-esteem, and a sense of purpose. This book, along with the other seven books in the **Adding Assets Series for Kids**, empowers young people ages 8–12 to build their own Developmental Assets.

But it's very important to acknowledge that building assets for and with young people is primarily an *adult* responsibility. What kids need most in their lives are grown-ups—parents and other relatives, teachers, school administrators, neighbors, youth leaders, religious leaders, community members, policy makers, advocates, and more—who care about them as individuals. They need adults who care enough to learn their names, to show interest in their lives, to listen when they talk, to provide them with opportunities to realize their potential, to teach them well, to give them sound advice, to serve as good examples, to guide them, to inspire them, to support them when they stumble, and to shield them from harm—as much as is humanly possible these days.

This book focuses on four of the 40 Developmental Assets identified by Search Institute. These are **External Assets**—positive experiences kids receive from the world around them. The four external assets described here are called the **Empowerment Assets.** Children are empowered when they are appreciated and valued by adults—not only their parents or other family members, but also adults in the larger community. They are empowered when they are perceived as having something meaningful to contribute, when they are given chances to help others, and when they feel safe from harm—when they're not threatened or victimized in their homes, schools, or neighborhoods.

Young people who have the empowerment assets know they are liked and respected. They're important and they belong. They matter to others, including grown-ups, as opposed to being "seen and not heard." This gives them the confidence to explore their own dreams, ideas, and opportunities. Because one of the most basic of all human needs is being met—the need for safety—they are free to grow and learn.

A list of all 40 Developmental Assets for middle childhood, with definitions, follows. If you want to know more about the assets, some of the resources listed on pages 67–68 will help you. Or you can visit the Search Institute Web site at *www.search-institute.org.*

Thank you for caring enough about kids to make this book available to the young person or persons in your life. We'd love to hear your success stories, and we welcome your suggestions for adding assets to kids' lives—or improving future editions of this book.

Pamela Espeland and Elizabeth Verdick
Free Spirit Publishing Inc.
217 Fifth Avenue North, Suite 200
Minneapolis, MN 55401-1299
help4kids@freespirit.com

The 40 Developmental Assets for Middle Childhood

EXTERNAL ASSETS

SUPPORT

1. **Family support**—Family life provides high levels of love and support.
2. **Positive family communication**—Parent(s) and child communicate positively. Child feels comfortable seeking advice and counsel from parent(s).
3. **Other adult relationships**—Child receives support from adults other than her or his parent(s).
4. **Caring neighborhood**—Child experiences caring neighbors.
5. **Caring school climate**—Relationships with teachers and peers provide a caring, encouraging school environment.
6. **Parent involvement in schooling**—Parent(s) are actively involved in helping the child succeed in school.

EMPOWERMENT

7. **Community values children**—Child feels valued and appreciated by adults in the community.
8. **Children as resources**—Child is included in decisions at home and in the community.
9. **Service to others**—Child has opportunities to help others in the community.
10. **Safety**—Child feels safe at home, at school, and in her or his neighborhood.

BOUNDARIES AND EXPECTATIONS

11. **Family boundaries**—Family has clear and consistent rules and consequences and monitors the child's whereabouts.
12. **School boundaries**—School provides clear rules and consequences.
13. **Neighborhood boundaries**—Neighbors take responsibility for monitoring the child's behavior.
14. **Adult role models**—Parents(s) and other adults in the child's family, as well as nonfamily adults, model positive, responsible behavior.
15. **Positive peer influence**—Child's closest friends model positive, responsible behavior.
16. **High expectations**—Parent(s) and teachers expect the child to do her or his best at school and in other activities.

CONSTRUCTIVE USE OF TIME

17. **Creative activities**—Child participates in music, art, drama, or creative writing two or more times per week.
18. **Child programs**—Child participates two or more times per week in cocurricular school activities or structured community programs for children.
19. **Religious community**—Child attends religious programs or services one or more times per week.
20. **Time at home**—Child spends some time most days both in high-quality interaction with parent(s) and doing things at home other than watching TV or playing video games.

INTERNAL ASSETS

COMMITMENT TO LEARNING

21. **Achievement motivation**—Child is motivated and strives to do well in school.
22. **Learning engagement**—Child is responsive, attentive, and actively engaged in learning at school and enjoys participating in learning activities outside of school.
23. **Homework**—Child usually hands in homework on time.
24. **Bonding to adults at school**—Child cares about teachers and other adults at school.
25. **Reading for pleasure**—Child enjoys and engages in reading for fun most days of the week.

POSITIVE VALUES

26. **Caring**—Parent(s) tell the child it is important to help other people.
27. **Equality and social justice**—Parent(s) tell the child it is important to speak up for equal rights for all people.
28. **Integrity**—Parent(s) tell the child it is important to stand up for one's beliefs.
29. **Honesty**—Parent(s) tell the child it is important to tell the truth.
30. **Responsibility**—Parent(s) tell the child it is important to accept personal responsibility for behavior.
31. **Healthy lifestyle**—Parent(s) tell the child it is important to have good health habits and an understanding of healthy sexuality.

SOCIAL COMPETENCIES

32. **Planning and decision making**—Child thinks about decisions and is usually happy with the results of her or his decisions.
33. **Interpersonal competence**—Child cares about and is affected by other people's feelings, enjoys making friends, and, when frustrated or angry, tries to calm herself or himself.
34. **Cultural competence**—Child knows and is comfortable with people of different racial, ethnic, and cultural backgrounds and with her or his own cultural identity.
35. **Resistance skills**—Child can stay away from people who are likely to get her or him in trouble and is able to say no to doing wrong or dangerous things.
36. **Peaceful conflict resolution**—Child attempts to resolve conflict nonviolently.

POSITIVE IDENTITY

37. **Personal power**—Child feels he or she has some influence over things that happen in her or his life.
38. **Self-esteem**—Child likes and is proud to be the person he or she is.
39. **Sense of purpose**—Child sometimes thinks about what life means and whether there is a purpose for her or his life.
40. **Positive view of personal future**—Child is optimistic about her or his personal future.

Helpful Resources

Books

Bullies Are a Pain in the Brain by Trevor Romain (Minneapolis: Free Spirit Publishing, 1997). Learn how to become "Bully-Proof," how to stop bullies from hurting others, and what to do in dangerous situations.

Reaching Your Goals by Robin Landew Silverman (New York: Franklin Watts, 2004). To turn a wish into a goal takes creative thinking and organized planning skills. This book shows how to make a plan and see it through to the end.

Stick Up for Yourself! Every Kid's Guide to Personal Power and Positive Self-Esteem by Gershen Kaufman, Ph.D., Lev Raphael, Ph.D., and Pamela Espeland (Minneapolis: Free Spirit Publishing, 1999). It's not always easy to say what's on your mind. With a focus on thinking positively and communicating emotions, this book includes tips and exercises to build confidence and make good choices.

Think for Yourself: A Kid's Guide to Solving Life's Dilemmas and Other Sticky Problems by Cynthia MacGregor (Toronto: Lobster Press, 2003). Daily problems are broken down into easy-to-follow categories: friends, family, grown-ups, and everyday situations. Real-life examples and choices for solutions reinforce the importance of thinking things through and doing what's best for you.

Web sites

Family Games
www.familygames.com
A great place to find fun, nonviolent games, quizzes, and software. Downloads are available plus links to more games, riddles, puzzles, and activities the whole family can enjoy.

National Youth Leadership Council (NYLC)
www.nylc.org
The NYLC brings kids, educators, and community leaders together to make sure that kids are seen, heard, and actively involved in community organizations and decision making.

Youth Service America
www.servenet.org
A helpful national resource to connect to organizations and service projects in your area. Type in your ZIP code, skills, and interests to find the best service experience for you.

Youth Venture
www.youthventure.org
Youth Venture believes every young person can make a difference. Do you have a solution to a problem in your community? Youth Venture invests in the ideas of young people who create, launch, and lead organizations, clubs, or businesses that provide a positive, lasting benefit in a school, neighborhood, or large community.

FOR ADULTS

Books

365 Ways to Raise Great Kids: Activities for Raising Bright, Caring, Honest, Respectful and Creative Children by Sheila Ellison and Barbara Ann Barnett (Naperville, IL: Sourcebooks, Incorporated, 1998). A resource for parents and educators filled with engaging, creative ways to help build self-esteem and strength of character in children.

Building Assets Is Elementary: Group Activities for Helping Kids Ages 8–12 Succeed by Search Institute (Minneapolis: Search Institute, 2004). Promoting creativity, time-management skills, kindness, manners, and more, this flexible activity book includes over 50 easy-to-use group exercises for the classroom or youth group.

The Bully Free Classroom™ by Allan L. Beane (Minneapolis: Free Spirit Publishing, 1999). More than 100 prevention and intervention strategies teachers and youth group leaders can use in the classroom, with victims, and with bullies themselves.

Our Family Meeting Book: Fun and Easy Ways to Manage Time, Build Communication, and Share Responsibility Week by Week by Elaine Hightower and Betsy Riley (Minneapolis: Free Spirit Publishing, 2002). Time management, long-range planning, and prioritizing skills are important assets for busy families. This book keeps many schedules organized and promotes open, effective communication within families.

What Kids Need to Succeed: Proven, Practical Ways to Raise Good Kids by Peter L. Benson, Ph.D., Judy Galbraith, M.A., and Pamela Espeland (Minneapolis: Free Spirit Publishing, 1994). More than 900 specific, concrete suggestions help adults help children build Developmental Assets at home, at school, and in the community.

What Young Children Need to Succeed: Working Together to Build Assets from Birth to Age 11 by Jolene L. Roehlkepartain and Nancy Leffert, Ph.D. (Minneapolis: Free Spirit Publishing, 2000). Hundreds of practical, concrete ideas help adults build Developmental Assets for children in four different age groups: birth to 12 months, and ages 1–2, 3–5, and 6–11. Includes inspiring true stories from across the United States.

Web sites

Alliance for Youth
www.americaspromise.org
Founded after the Presidents' Summit for America's Future in 1997, this organization is committed to fulfilling five promises to American youth: Every child needs *caring adults, safe places,* a *healthy start, marketable skills,* and *opportunities to serve.* This collaborative network includes resources, information, and opportunities for involvement.

Connect for Kids
www.connectforkids.org
Tips, articles, resources, volunteer opportunities, and more for adults who want to improve the lives of children in their community and beyond. Includes the complete text of Richard Louv's book *101 Things You Can Do for Our Children's Future.*

National Mentoring Partnership
www.mentoring.org
The organization provides connections, training, resources, and advice to introduce and support mentoring partnerships. The site is a wealth of information about becoming and finding a mentor.

Search Institute
www.search-institute.org
Through dynamic research and analysis, this independent nonprofit organization works to promote healthy, active, and content youth and communities.

Index

About the Authors

Both Pamela Espeland and Elizabeth Verdick have written many books for children and teens.

Pamela is the coauthor (with Peter L. Benson and Judy Galbraith) of *What Kids Need to Succeed* and *What Teens Need to Succeed* and the author of *Succeed Every Day*, all based on Search Institute's concept of the 40 Developmental Assets. She is the author of *Life Lists for Teens* and the coauthor (with Gershen Kaufman and Lev Raphael) of *Stick Up for Yourself!*

Elizabeth is a children's book writer and editor. She is the author of *Teeth Are Not for Biting, Words Are Not for Hurting,* and *Feet Are Not for Kicking* and coauthor (with Marjorie Lisovskis) of *How to Take the GRRRR Out of Anger* and (with Trevor Romain) of *Stress Can Really Get on Your Nerves* and *True or False? Tests Stink!*

Pamela and Elizabeth first worked together on *Making Every Day Count*. They live in Minnesota with their families and pets.

More Titles in the Adding Assets Series for Kids

Each book is 80–100 pages, softcover, two-color illustrations, 5⅛" x 7", $9.95. For ages 8–12.

People Who Care About You
Kids build the six Support Assets: Family Support, Positive Family Communication, Other Adult Relationships, Caring Neighborhood, Caring School Climate, and Parent Involvement in Schooling.

Doing and Being Your Best
Kids build the six Boundaries and Expectations Assets: Family Boundaries, School Boundaries, Neighborhood Boundaries, Adult Role Models, Positive Peer Influence, and High Expectations.

Smart Ways to Spend Your Time
Kids build the four Constructive Use of Time Assets: Creative Activities, Child Programs, Religious Community, and Time at Home.

Loving to Learn

Kids build the five Commitment to Learning Assets: Achievement Motivation, Learning Engagement, Homework, Bonding to Adults at School, and Reading for Pleasure.

Knowing and Doing What's Right

Kids build the six Positive Values Assets: Caring, Equality and Social Justice, Integrity, Honesty, Responsibility, and Healthy Lifestyle.

Making Choices and Making Friends

Kids build the five Social Competencies Assets: Planning and Decision Making, Interpersonal Competence, Cultural Competence, Resistance Skills, and Peaceful Conflict Resolution.

Proud to Be You
Kids build the four Positive Identity Assets: Personal Power, Self-Esteem, Sense of Purpose, and Positive View of Personal Future.

A Leader's Guide to The Adding Assets Series for Kids
A comprehensive, easy-to-use curriculum for building all 40 Developmental Assets, with activities, discussion prompts, handouts for parents and other family adults, and a scope-and-sequence for standards-based education. The included CD-ROM features all of the reproducible forms from the book and an additional 40 pages of student handouts used in the sessions. For grades 3–6.

$39.95; 288 pp.; softcover; lay-flat binding; 8½" x 11".

To place an order or to request a free catalog of SELF-HELP FOR KIDS® and SELF-HELP FOR TEENS® materials, please write, call, email, or visit our Web site:

Free Spirit Publishing Inc.
217 Fifth Avenue North • Suite 200 • Minneapolis, MN 55401-1299
toll-free 800.735.7323 • local 612.338.2068 • fax 612.337.5050
help4kids@freespirit.com • www.freespirit.com

Fast, Friendly, and Easy to Use

www.freespirit.com

Browse the catalog

Info & extras

Many ways to search

Quick check-out

Stop in and see!

Our fresh new Web site makes it easier than ever to find the positive, reliable resources you need to empower teens and kids of all ages.

The Catalog.
Start browsing with just one click.

Beyond the Home Page.
Information and extras such as links and downloads.

The Search Box.
Find anything superfast.

Your Voice.
See testimonials from customers like you.

Request the Catalog.
Browse our catalog on paper, too!

The Nitty-Gritty.
Toll-free numbers, online ordering information, and more.

The 411.
News, reviews, awards, and special events.

Our Web site is a secure commerce site. All of the personal information you enter at our site—including your name, address, and credit card number—is secure. So you can order with confidence when you order online from Free Spirit!

For a fast and easy way to receive our practical tips, helpful information, and special offers, send your email address to upbeatnews@freespirit.com. View a sample letter and our privacy policy at *www.freespirit.com.*

1.800.735.7323 • fax 612.337.5050 • help4kids@freespirit.com